THE SECRET INGREDIENT

THE SECRET INGREDIENT

THE MYSTERY WRITERS' COOKBOOK

edited by Dawn Dowdle

LEVEL BEST BOOKS

First published by Level Best Books 2021

Copyright © 2021 by Dawn Dowdle, Editor

All rights reserved. No part of this publication may be reproduced, stored or transmitted in any form or by any means, electronic, mechanical, photocopying, recording, scanning, or otherwise without written permission from the publisher. It is illegal to copy this book, post it to a website, or distribute it by any other means without permission.

Dawn Dowdle, Editor asserts the moral right to be identified as the author of this work.

First edition

Cover art by Level Best Designs

This book was professionally typeset on Reedsy.
Find out more at reedsy.com

To our readers who make writing such a delight.

Contents

Index by Author   v

I   Victoria Justice Mysteries

Victoria Justice Mysteries by Andrea J. Johnson	3
Ian Cooper's Killer Crab Cakes	5
Jillian Gailbraith's Hip Brit Scones	8

II   Cleo Mack Mysteries

Cleo Mack Mysteries by G.P. Gardner	13
Veggie Chukker Chili*	15
Roasted Veggies	17

III   Brenna Flynn Mysteries

Brenna Flynn Mysteries by Rose Kerr	21
Rose Kerr's Hearty Chicken Soup	23

IV   On Pointe Mystery Series

On Pointe Mysteries by Lori Robbins	29
Spinach Noodles with Spinach	31

V Maggie White Mystery Series

Maggie White Mysteries by Jen Collins Moore — 35
Maggie White's 6-Ingredient Toasted Gnocchi — 36

VI The Chesapeake Bay Mysteries

The Chesapeake Bay Mysteries by Judy L Murray — 41
Linguini and Clams — 43

VII Cassie Gwynne Mysteries

Cassie Gwynne Mysteries by Genevieve Essig — 49
Aunt Flora's Orange Blossom Scones — 51
Candied Orange Peels — 53

VIII Laura Bishop Mysteries

Laura Bishop Mysteries by Grace Topping — 57
English Sherry Trifle — 59

IX Cabin by the Lake Mysteries

Cabin by the Lake Mysteries by Linda Norlander — 65
Jamie's Hearty Beef Stew and Vegetables — 67

X Haunted Library Mysteries

Haunted Library Mysteries by Allison Brook — 71
Marilyn's Veggie and Cheese Casserole — 73

XI Tory Benning Mystery Series

Tory Benning Mysteries by Judith Gonda   77
Uncle Bob's Christmas Trifle   78

XII All-Day Breakfast Café Mysteries

All-Day Breakfast Café Mysteries by Lena Gregory   83
Gia's Home Fries   85

XIII Cupcake Catering Mystery Series

Cupcake Catering Mysteries by Kim Davis   89
Tropical Pineapple Muffins   90
Choco-Colada Cocktail Cupcakes   93
Choco-Colada Cocktail   97

XIV Low Country Dog Walker Mysteries

Low Country Dog Walker Mysteries by Jackie Layton   101
Andi Grace Scott's Puppy Chow   103
Juliet's Chocolate Bars   105
Marc's Sunshine Smoothie   107

XV Jules Keene Glamping Mysteries

Jules Keene Glamping Mysteries by Heather Weidner   111
Chocolaty Éclair Pies   113

XVI Washington Whodunit Mysteries

Washington Whodunit Mysteries by Colleen J. Shogan 117
Pepperoni Bread   119

Acknowledgements

Index by Author

- Haunted Library Mysteries by Allison Brook
- Cupcake Catering Mysteries by Kim Davis
- Cassie Geynne Mysteries by Genevieve Essig
- Cleo Mack Mysteries by G.P. Gardner
- Tory Benning Mysteries by Judith Gonda
- All-Day Breakfast Café Mysteries by Lena Gregory
- Victoria Justice Mysteries by Andrea J. Johnson
- Brenna Flynn Mysteries by Rose Kerr
- Low Country Dog Walker Mysteries by Jackie Layton
- Maggie White Mysteries by Jen Collins Moore
- The Chesapeake Bay Mysteries by Judy L. Murray
- Cabin by the Lake Mysteries by Linda Norlander
- On Pointe Mysteries by Lori Robbins
- Washington Whodunit Mysteries by Colleen J. Shogan
- Laura Bishop Mysteries by Grace Topping
- Jules Keene Glamping Mysteries by Heather Weidne

I

Victoria Justice Mysteries

Victoria Justice Mysteries by Andrea J. Johnson

Poetic Justice
Deceptive Justice

Polis Books (Agora Imprint)

A brilliant, no-nonsense heroine of color dares to answer the question "What if the silent but all-seeing court stenographer, not the cops or the attorneys, solved the murder and saved the day?" Set against the colorful backdrop of the famed Delmarva Peninsula in the fictional seaside hamlet of Bickerton, Delaware, each book highlights the regional flavor of Victoria's rural homestead through unique events, like the Apple-Scrapple Carnival and the Post-Election Festival, and exposes readers to the unique world of shorthand stenography. Victoria uses the tools of her trade to unravel her community's dark secrets, with the help of a diverse cast of quirky characters, such as the brash seafood restauranter Ian Cooper and the sweet British café owner Jillian Gailbraith, whose recipes are the talk of the town.

Andrea J. Johnson is a writer and editor whose expertise lies in traditional mysteries and romance. She holds an M.F.A. in Writing Popular Fiction from Seton Hill University and a copyediting certification from U.C. San Diego. Her craft essays have appeared on several websites, such as *Litreactor*,

DIY MFA, *Submittable*, and *Funds for Writers*. She also writes entertainment articles for the women's lifestyle websites *Popsugar* and *The List Daily*. Learn more about Andrea and her series at ajthenovelist.com.

Ian Cooper's Killer Crab Cakes

Serves 6

Ingredients:

- 10 butter crackers
- 2 tablespoons mayonnaise
- 2 teaspoons Old Bay
- 1 teaspoon fresh minced parsley
- 1 teaspoon fresh minced cilantro
- 1 teaspoon Dijon mustard
- 1 teaspoon Worcestershire sauce
- 1 pinch salt

- ½ teaspoon lemon juice
- 1 egg
- 1 pound jumbo lump crab meat
- 2 tablespoons salted butter or nonstick cooking spray (for frying or baking)

Instructions:

1. Place all 10 butter crackers into a plastic bag and crush them into a fine powder. Set aside.
2. Add the mayonnaise, Old Bay, parsley, cilantro, Dijon mustard, Worcestershire sauce, salt, lemon juice, and egg into a large mixing bowl. Whisk until the spice mixture is silky.
3. Place the jumbo lump crab meat on top of the spice mixture and pour the crushed crackers on top of the crab.
4. Fold the crab and crackers into the spice mixture to combine the ingredients. Do this slowly and with a soft spatula (or your hands) to avoid breaking the lumps of meat. Limit the folds to as few turns as possible—do not overwork the mixture.
5. Cover the bowl and place the finished product in the refrigerator for at least 30 minutes—but no more than 24 hours. This will help flavors comingle and ensure your cake stays together during the cooking process.
6. Preheat the broiler and grease the baking sheet with butter or a nonstick cooking spray.
7. Form the finished product into six equal-sized patties and gently place them on the buttered baking sheet. Leave at least 2 inches between each crab cake.
8. Broil for 10-15 minutes or until golden brown. (If your oven doesn't broil, bake at 450°F for 15-18 minutes.) Do not touch or turn. Crab cakes are meant to be crispy, but they will remain delicate. Avoid unnecessary manhandling during the cook time, unless you want a mess.

9. Cool 10 minutes before removing from the pan. Serve warm with a side salad or a fresh piece of cornbread.

This is not a recipe for anyone who likes to substitute ingredients. True downhome crab cakes, akin to those on the Delmarva Peninsula, have lots of meat with very little filler and are known for their smoky Old Bay flavor. Therefore, the first order of business is to locate the trademarked seasoning on your spice aisle. Imitators will not cut it.

Butter crackers are also essential in creating a signature Delmarva crab cake with a creamy flavor. Use the no-name brands if you must, but do not substitute this ingredient for saltines, soda crackers, or white bread. You're just setting yourself up for a bland meal. Also, don't be tempted to add more crackers. A winning crab cake bursts with quality meat—that's why jumbo lump blue crab is the choice of champions. Avoid the stringy claw meat or the less sweet backfin fare some grocers try to ply on unsuspecting customers.

Last, but not least, don't get cute and add vegetables. Keep the focus on the crustacean. This is not the time to add avocado, carrots, onions, garlic, or celery. Crab has a sweet delicate flavor that can be quickly overpowered by such items. Ditch the veggies and stick with the herbs listed because they have been curated to enhance the unique flavor of the crab. Dried varieties of parsley and cilantro are sufficient, but go fresh when possible. Remember, the whole point of this recipe's green ingredients is to revive the seafood's freshness, so splurge on real herbs. You won't regret it.

Some final pointers for burgeoning crab cake chefs:

If you must cook your crab cakes on the stovetop, make sure the skillet is scorching hot and coated with butter before putting the crab cakes in, two at a time. Do not overcrowd the pan as it will reduce the heat and lead to uneven results. Don't smash the crab cakes as they cook, and don't fiddle with them. Assuming your skillet is hot enough, 4 minutes per side is sufficient. You want the surface of the cake to turn gold or brown and form a crust. Perfect cakes are crunchy on the outside and oo-la-la unctuous on the inside.

Jillian Gailbraith's Hip Brit Scones

Serves 12

Ingredients:

- 3 cups cake flour
- ⅓ cup sugar
- 2 teaspoons baking powder
- 1 teaspoon baking soda
- ½ teaspoon salt
- 6 tablespoons cold unsalted butter
- ½ cup milk
- 3 tablespoons lemon juice

- 1 teaspoon white vinegar
- 1 egg yolk beaten with 1 tablespoon milk (for color)

Instructions:

1. Preheat the oven to 350°.
2. Sift the flour, sugar, baking powder, baking soda, and salt into a mixing bowl.
3. Dice the butter into cubes and add them to the dry ingredients. Use a pastry cutter to combine the ingredients until the mixture crumbles.
4. In a separate bowl or cup, whisk the milk, lemon juice, and vinegar together. Pour the liquid mixture into the dry mixture.
5. Use a rubber spatula to combine the ingredients until a wet dough forms.
6. Lightly flour a flat surface and pour the dough on top. Turn and knead the dough, flattening out a surface that's about one-inch thick. Be careful not to overwork the dough.
7. Cut 2-inch circles using a well-floured cookie cutter or the mouth of a wide glass.
8. Place the circles on a baking sheet that has been greased and floured. Brush each with the egg yolk and milk mixture prior to baking so they brown as they cook.
9. Bake the scones for 12-15 minutes. Allow at least 10 minutes to cool. Serve warm with a mug of ginger-lemon tea.

Authentic British scones are a scary thing for most Americans. At first glance, many mistake them for biscuits, while others scoff they're not glazed in sugar like the ones found at those coffee-centric fast-food chains. Here's the truth: A real British scone is meant as a light snack designed to tide you over between lunch and dinner. Therefore, they're not intended to be sickeningly sweet, like a standard pastry, and they're also much denser than your typical honeybun or donut. Scones are hearty, almost neutral in taste, and tough enough to stand on their own. That's what makes them the perfect accompaniment to a cup of fresh-brewed tea. If you need something with a little more sweetness, load your scone with jam and clotted cream—or for you American lads and lassies, preserves and butter will work just as well.

II

Cleo Mack Mysteries

Cleo Mack Mysteries by G.P. Gardner

Murder at Harbor Village
Murder at Royale Court
Murder at the Arts & Crafts Festival

Lyrical Underground

Cleo Mack is a social worker at a Georgia university when she's offered a sweet buyout if she'll retire immediately. In *Murder at Harbor Village*, a *U.S.A. Today* best seller, Cleo moves to a quaint little town near Alabama's gulf coast, expecting to work part-time at a community for active seniors. But the community falls apart when its director is murdered. Cleo is persuaded to take the director's job, solve the murder, and steer the community back to stability.

In *Murder at Royale Court*, Cleo and a Harbor Village resident discover a body in the Royale Court shopping center. Cleo solves the murder, attracts the attention of a mysteriously private retiree, and competes with her ex-husband in a trivia contest staged during the town's first antique automobile show.

In *Murder at the Arts & Crafts Festival*, portrait artist Twinkle Thaw drops dead, mysteriously poisoned, while attending a birthday party at—you guessed it—Harbor Village. Cleo solves the murder after connecting it to a decades-old art heist. Her new beau renovates a house in hopes she'll move in with him, and his flamboyant interior decorator decides the community simply must acquire a major art collection, which he intends to select.

G.P. Gardner writes mysteries set in the South. She has degrees in psychology and business and continues to study topics that appeal to her—pottery, knitting, photorealistic drawing, and genealogy, at the moment—and incorporates those interests into her writing. A native of Alabama, she has lived in Georgia, Tennessee, South Carolina, and—oops!—Wisconsin, where she learned she's definitely more the tropical type. She now lives in Fairhope, Alabama, a quaint and charming town before it turned into a hurricane magnet, and usually follows a vegetarian diet. She is a member of Sisters in Crime. You can find her on Facebook as GP Gardner or at www.GPGardner.com.

Veggie Chukker Chili*

Serves 5-6

Ingredients:

- 2 tablespoons olive oil
- 2 medium onions, chopped
- 1 carrot, peeled & chopped
- 2 15-oz cans dark red kidney beans, drained & rinsed
- 15-oz can black beans, drained & rinsed
- 15-oz can diced tomatoes, with liquid
- Approximately half of a 28-oz can crushed tomatoes
- Chili seasoning packet, any brand, mild or hot

- 1 bag beefless crumbles, about 13 ounces (Morningstar Farms, Boca, or other brand)
- 1 cup frozen corn kernels
- 4-ounce can mild diced green chilies
- ¼ cup mild or hot tomato salsa,
- 3-4 cups water
- Corn chips or crackers
- Optional extras: Chopped green onions, Shredded cheddar cheese, Sour cream

Instructions:

1. In stockpot, heat olive oil.
2. Add onions and carrot.
3. Sauté until onion is transparent.
4. Add beans, tomatoes, chili seasoning, crumbles, corn, chilies, salsa and water. Bring to a boil. Cover on lower heat and simmer for at least an hour, stirring occasionally.

Serve with corn chips or crackers plus your choice of options.

Like most chili, it's even better reheated a day or two later and is especially tasty served over a big scoop of hot rice. You may need to add water to adjust the thickness.

*Named for The Chukker, a University of Alabama student hangout in the old days.

Roasted Veggies

Serves 4-5 as a main dish

Ingredients:

- 24-ounce bag Honey Gold baby potatoes
- 2 bell peppers, any color
- 2 medium zucchinis
- 3 carrots
- 12 cherry tomatoes
- 5 medium yellow onions
- 3 tablespoons olive oil
- 6 grinds sea salt

- 10-12 grinds pepper
- 1 tablespoon dried basil
- ¼ cup Parmesan or mixed Italian cheeses, grated
- Optional: balsamic vinegar when serving

Instructions:

1. Preheat oven to 400º.
2. Wash potatoes, bell peppers, zucchini, carrots, and tomatoes.
3. Quarter the potatoes and add to a large bowl.
4. Peel onions, slice into 6 or 8 pieces, and add to the bowl.
5. Halve bell peppers, discard stem and seeds, chop into 1-inch pieces, and add to bowl.
6. Slice zucchini vertically into 6 or 8 wedges, discarding stem. Then slice wedges into 1-inch pieces. Add to bowl.
7. Peel carrots, slice into half-inch rounds, and add to bowl.
8. Add cherry tomatoes to bowl.
9. Pour olive oil over the veggies. Add salt, pepper and dried basil. Stir to mix well.
10. Transfer to baking dish or pan and bake, uncovered.
11. After 30 minutes, add the grated cheese and stir again.
12. Bake for another 30 minutes, or until potatoes and onions begin to brown along edges and are soft when pierced with a fork.
13. Balsamic vinegar is optional at serving.

III

Brenna Flynn Mysteries

Brenna Flynn Mysteries by Rose Kerr

Death on the Set
Death in Academia
Death at the Festival

TouchPoint Press

Set in the fictional town of Bayview City, in the Upper Peninsula of Michigan, the Brenna Flynn Mysteries follow our amateur sleuth as she rebuilds her life.

Brenna Flynn's life plan isn't working out the way it's supposed to. In her early 30s, she and her husband should be planning a family and her work as a high school guidance counselor providing her with personal and professional satisfaction. Instead, in four short months, her life was upended. Her husband was killed in a car accident, she learned he's kept some dark secrets from her, and then, she was downsized from her job.

With no other options, Brenna returns home to Bayview City to pick up the pieces of her life. With the help of a family friend, who owns a temp agency, Brenna finds work. In the first book, she finds work as a production assistant on a cooking reality T.V. show. In the second book, she's working at the university in the research department. In the third book, Brenna is employed in the Special Events office for Bayview City. Brenna enjoys the challenges each new position delivers, but finding murdered victims isn't supposed to be part of the job description.

Suspicion falls on Brenna or members of her family. Determined to prove she or the accused are innocent, Brenna gathers information about the victims and the people in their lives. Using the skills honed as a counsellor, Brenna is able to discover information. People talk to her and let their guard down because she isn't a police officer. Brenna curates the information, makes deductions, and shares them with a certain private investigator and the police. This provides the police with information that allows them to find the killer.

Rose Kerr grew up in a small town in Nova Scotia, Canada. She discovered mystery books at a young age, and Agatha Christie was a favorite author.

She and her husband raised their family in a small town in Northern Ontario on the shores of Lake Superior. The town and several other communities provided inspiration for the fictional town of Bayview City, where the Brenna Flynn series takes place.

A former distance education administrator, she is happy following her passion for mysteries with her writing.

Rose is a member of Sisters in Crime and the online Guppy Chapter of Sisters in Crime.

She and her husband now make their home in Southern Ontario.

Rose Kerr's Hearty Chicken Soup

Serves 12-14

This soup will warm you up on a cold winter's day. It's thick and hearty. Turkey may be substituted for chicken.

Stock Ingredients:

- Chicken carcass
- 2 cloves garlic, chopped
- 1 bay leaf
- 1 teaspoon summer savory*
- 1 teaspoon salt

- 1 teaspoon pepper
- ½ cup carrots, chopped coarsely
- ½ cup onion, chopped coarsely
- 3 celery stalks (with leaves), chopped coarsely
- 10 cups water

Soup Ingredients:

- 9 cups chicken stock (homemade is best, but store-bought will do)
- 1 can (10 ½ ounces) condensed tomato soup
- 1 envelope dry onion soup mix
- 2 cups water
- 1 cup dry soup mix (lentils, barley, green split peas, yellow split peas)
- 2 bay leaves
- ½-1 teaspoon summer savory
- ½ teaspoon black pepper
- 2 cloves garlic or 1 teaspoon chopped garlic
- 1 cup diced red peppers
- 1 cup diced green peppers
- ½ cup corn niblets
- 2 cups diced cooked chicken or turkey
- 1 cup baby pasta shells, macaroni, or rice

*Summer savory is an herb in the mint family.
https://www.savoryspiceshop.com/savory-summer

Homemade stock Instructions:

1. In a large pot, add the chicken carcass, garlic, bay leaf, summer savory, salt, pepper, carrots, onion, and celery. Cover completely with water.
2. Bring ingredients to a boil, then lower heat to simmer. Allow to simmer

for 2-3 hours, or until the meat falls off the bone. Please note, carcass must be covered in water. Add ½ cup water at a time if needed.
3. Using a colander or strainer, drain the stock into a large bowl or pot.
4. While stock is cooling, remove any meat from the chicken and dice into small pieces.
5. Once the stock is cooled, remove any visible fat from the stock.

Soup Instructions:

1. In a large pot, add the chicken stock, tomato soup, onion soup mix, and water.
2. Stir well and bring to a boil.
3. Add soup mix, bay leaves, summer savory, pepper, and garlic. Stir gently. Reduce heat to low and allow the soup to simmer for 2 hours, stirring occasionally. Taste and adjust accordingly, adding more summer savory, black pepper, or garlic as needed.
4. Add red and green peppers, corn, and diced cooked chicken. Stir mixture and allow to simmer for another ½ hour. Stirring often.
5. Add baby pasta shells, macaroni, or rice. Mix well. Simmer for another ½ hour or until pasta or is cooked. Stir often. Soup will be thick.

Serve with fresh homemade bread or buns.

IV

On Pointe Mystery Series

On Pointe Mysteries by Lori Robbins

Murder in First Position
Murder in Second Position
Murder in Third Position

Level Best Books

Everything is beautiful at the ballet—until it isn't. When backstage intrigue, blackmail, and a tangle of romantic liaisons result in murder, ballerina Leah Siderova has to pull back the curtain on the deadlier side of dance.

Ballet, with its merciless discipline, is all she's ever known. Will that be enough to save her and those she loves? Only one thing is certain: with grit and wit, Leah learns there's more to life—and to her—than being center stage.

Note: Because Leah never cooks, and thinks coffee and diet soda are essential food groups, she had no recipes to share. But her perfect and perfectly wonderful sister stepped in to help her out. After all, what are sisters for, if not to help you hide from the police, foil a murder plot, and cook beautiful meals in their spare time?

Brooklyn-born Lori Robbins began dancing at age sixteen and launched her professional career three years later. After ten very lean years as a dancer, she attended Hunter College, graduating summa cum laude with a major in British Literature and a minor in Classics. The first book in her On Pointe Mystery series, *Murder in First Position*, won the Indie Award for Best Mystery.

The first book in her Master Class Mystery series, *Lesson Plan for Murder*, won the Silver Falchion Award for Best Cozy Mystery and was a finalist in the Readers' Choice and Indie Book Awards.

Robbins is currently working on the sequel to both books. Her short story, "Accidents Happen," is in the *Murder Most Diabolical* anthology, and "Leading Ladies" will appear in the New York Sisters in Crime anthology, *Justice for All*. She is a past vice-president of the New York chapter of Sisters in Crime and a member of Mystery Writers of America and International Thriller Writers. Robbins is an expert in the homicidal impulses everyday life inspires. Find her at lorirobbins.com or on Facebook and Instagram at LoriRobbinsMysteries.

Spinach Noodles with Spinach

Serves 4

Ingredients:

- 1 box (12 ounces) spinach fettuccine (or any pasta you have, though something colorful is nice)
- 1-2 tablespoons olive oil
- 1 small onion, thinly sliced
- 1 cup sliced mushrooms
- 1-2 cloves minced garlic
- One bunch fresh spinach
- ½ cup (or more, to taste) plain yogurt or sour cream

- ¼ cup Parmesan cheese (plus more for serving)
- Salt and pepper to taste
- A pinch of nutmeg (optional)
- 5+ leaves minced fresh basil (optional)

Instructions:

1. Cook pasta according to package directions.
2. While the pasta cooks, heat olive oil in deep skillet or pot.
3. Add onion, mushrooms, and garlic and sauté lightly.
4. Add spinach, cover, and cook until spinach is wilted.
5. Drain excess water from the cooked spinach.
6. Add cooked pasta.
7. Add yogurt, Parmesan cheese, salt, and pepper to taste and mix well.
8. Let cook, covered, for a minute or 2 and add basil and/or nutmeg, if desired.

V

Maggie White Mystery Series

Maggie White Mysteries by Jen Collins Moore

Murder in the Piazza
Murder in Trastevere
Murder on the Appian Way

Level Best Books

A downsized American executive stuck in Rome on her husband's expat assignment thinks offering painting instruction to well-heeled travelers will unlock the secret to living the *dolce vita*. But when she discovers murder, Maggie White can't resist getting involved.

Jen Collins Moore transports readers to Rome in her new series, the Maggie White Mysteries. The perfect blend of funny and smart, Jen's debut novel, *Murder in the Piazza*, is filled with the art, history and food of Europe's greatest city. The founder of Meet Meals, Jen lives in Chicago with her husband and two sons.

Maggie White's 6-Ingredient Toasted Gnocchi

Serves 3

Gnocchi is one of Italy's most delicious contributions to global cuisine, and that's saying a lot for the country that invented pizza, pasta, and gelato. But it turns out those pillowy potato dumplings get even more delicious when you toast them. No boiling required, just a hot oven and a drizzle of olive oil and you've got the foundation for a seriously great meal. My favorite pairing: tossed with fresh spinach, crumbled gorgonzola, and toasted pine nuts. It's a six-ingredient dinner that's on the table in less than 30 minutes.

MAGGIE WHITE'S 6-INGREDIENT TOASTED GNOCCHI

Ingredients:

- 1 17.6-ounce package shelf-stable gnocchi
- Olive oil
- Salt and Pepper
- 1 to 2 cloves garlic (vary to your preference), minced
- 5 ounces baby spinach
- 3 ounces gorgonzola
- 2 tablespoons pine nuts, toasted
- ½ lemon

Instructions:

1. Preheat your oven to 425°.
2. Toss the gnocchi with olive oil, salt, and pepper in a large bowl and arrange on a rimmed baking sheet in a single layer.
3. Cook until golden brown, about 22-25 minutes, stirring once midway through.
4. When the gnocchi is just about ready, heat 2 tablespoons olive oil over medium heat in a large skillet.
5. Add the minced garlic (1 clove if you like a little garlic and 2 cloves if you like more) until fragrant, about 30 seconds.
6. Add the spinach and cook for 1 minute then transfer to the large mixing bowl.
7. Add the toasted gnocchi, gorgonzola, and pine nuts.
8. Toss well so the spinach continues to wilt a bit then add a squeeze of lemon.
9. Taste and add more lemon, salt, or pepper as needed. Enjoy!

VI

The Chesapeake Bay Mysteries

The Chesapeake Bay Mysteries by Judy L Murray

Murder in the Master
Murder in the Kitchen
Murder in the Pool House

Level Best Books

The Chesapeake Bay Mystery Series introduces recent widow Realtor Helen Morrisey. She is quick-witted and determined, and, like many mature women, she's trying hard to figure out what she needs in friends, family, men, and life in general. She is stubborn and hates taking orders. She loves to eat but never cooks. Her go-to food is Twizzlers.

First in the series is Murder in the Master. Thrown into a murder investigation with two friends desperate to find the culprit, Helen decides to create her own private Detection Club. Much like the club of Agatha Christie in the 1930s, Helen starts consulting her favorite sleuths – Miss Marple, Agatha Raisin, Nancy Drew, Jessica Fletcher, and Nora Charles. Helen's friends and a hunky detective may find her methods unusual but admit they are effective. Detective Joe McAlister decides to take advantage of her insight into back-office real estate deals and small bay town local players but quickly realizes he's losing control. He's falling fast. The fact that sharp-tongued Helen is resistant to romance and focused on crime only adds to his frustration and readers' fun.

A Philadelphia real estate broker and restoration addict, Judy Murray has worked with enough delusional sellers, jittery buyers, testy contractors, and diva agents to fill her head with back-office insight and gossip. Judy lives atop a cliff on the Chesapeake Bay, where she writes long after sunset. She is buffeted by winds in winter and invaded by family and dogs in summer. Judy is a member of Sisters in Crime and Mystery Writers of America. Find her at www.judylmurraymysteries.com and Facebook.

Linguini and Clams

Serves 8

If Helen was a good cook, which she is not, she would reach for this recipe and deceive her guests. She loves pasta and she loves a meal that says "fresh." Everyone will think you've spent hours when you actually spent minutes. I guarantee they'll say "Wow."

Ingredients:

- 1 bag fresh littleneck clams
- 1 tablespoon salt
- Olive oil

THE SECRET INGREDIENT

- 5 cloves garlic
- 1 ½ pounds linguini
- Dash of white wine (about ¼ cup)—whatever is open—not Riesling.
- ½ teaspoon red pepper flakes
- ½ cup fresh parsley, chopped
- 1 teaspoon black pepper
- 5 cans chopped clams
- 1 cup fresh parsley

Instructions:

1. Let your clams soak in a water bath. Drain, Rinse. Soak again. Drain, Rinse. Set aside.
2. Boil water for pasta. Add a tablespoon of salt.
3. In a large deep skillet, add a dash of olive oil and toss in the garlic.
4. Add the juice from the cans of clams. Don't put the chopped clams in yet or they'll get chewy.
5. Add a dash of your white wine.
6. Add red pepper flakes
7. Add chopped parsley
8. Add black pepper
9. Add your fresh clams to the deep skillet with the garlic and cover. Let the juices come out and the clams open.
10. Add the pasta into the pot.
11. A note on the pasta: Test your pasta after a few minutes. When it seems ALMOST done, it will continue to cook. Remove from heat and strain, reserving a cup of the pasta water.
12. Pour the pasta back into the pasta pot and add the cup of pasta water back onto the pasta and a dash of olive oil.
13. Note: Taste the plain pasta! I like to add a little Crazy Jane (Crazy Jane's mixed-up salt—found in the seasoning aisle) OR you can follow my thrifty example and buy on Amazon by the caseload. Great stocking

stuffer, by the way.
14. Pour the pasta into your serving dish.
15. Now take your sauce (do a final taste to see if you need any more seasoning) and pour over the pasta, spreading the clams evenly.
16. Sprinkle a cup of fresh parsley all over and serve HOT HOT HOT with a fresh baguette.
17. Pour yourself a glass of Sauvignon Blanc and enjoy the raving compliments.

VII

Cassie Gwynne Mysteries

Cassie Gwynne Mysteries by Genevieve Essig

Book 1 - A Deception Most Deadly
Book 2 - Title TBD
Book 3 - Title TBD

Bookouture/Storyfire Limited, a member of Hachette UK

Set in the 1880s Fernandina, on Amelia Island, Florida, this lighthearted but heartfelt series takes readers to a place far less traveled in literature than the Victorian-era American cities usually written about. Dubbed the "Newport of the South" and the "Island City" by contemporary travel publications, Fernandina enjoyed its own short but significant Golden Age during these years as not only an important rail and shipping crossroads but also a popular retreat for well-heeled tourists, including members of the Carnegie, Du Pont, and Vanderbilt families. At the same time, Florida, which has always been an outsider to the rest of the country and therefore a haven for outsiders as well— including, at various points in history, persecuted monks, British settlers fleeing the Revolution, pirates, escaped slaves, consumptives, and itinerant "cracker cowboys"—still had a touch of the wild about it. And late-nineteenth-century Fernandina, a place where the glittering social elite and patrons of rough-and-tumble saloons shared the shade of the same palm trees, was no different.

The series begins as Cassie Gwynne, still struggling to cope with her father's death, travels to Fernandina to meet her newfound aunt, a local perfumer named Flora Hale. Shortly after arrival, however, she discovers Flora's most-hated neighbor, a cantankerous harbor pilot, dead at the foot of the harbor pilots' lookout tower. When a less-than-objective coroner's jury accuses Flora of his murder, Cassie, aided by Flora's quirky group of friends—including a foul-mouthed curiosities shop owner, a blind Civil War veteran, a half-Chinese newspaper boy, and even a three-legged dog—must confront her doubts about her mysterious aunt and solve the case, or risk losing the only family she has left. Along the way, Cassie realizes there is a lot about her family, and her father, she never knew. She also starts to question whether the mugging which resulted in her father's death the year before was actually a random act of violence.

Florida-raised, Yale- and UVA-educated, and Chicago buffed and polished, Genevieve currently calls New Orleans home. When she's not writing or practicing law, she enjoys shooting pool, performing in operas and musicals, ogling historic buildings, acting for film and television, futzing with inventions that address highly specific and possibly only-annoying-to-her problems, traveling, ranting at bartenders about the evils of straws, horseback riding, and petting strange cats. Follow her on Facebook/Instagram (@essigauthor) or at genevieveessig.com.

Aunt Flora's Orange Blossom Scones

Makes 8 scones

Cassie's newfound aunt, Flora, bakes these scones on the first morning Cassie wakes up on the island. Flora is a perfumer known for her neroli and orange blossom scents, so this delicate, aromatic recipe features orange blossom water reserved from her still, along with candied orange peels made from fruit picked in her orchards.

Ingredients:

- 2 cups flour
- 3 tablespoons sugar

- 4 teaspoons baking powder
- ½ teaspoon salt
- ½ teaspoon nutmeg
- ¼ cup shredded, unsweetened coconut
- 3 tablespoons unrefined coconut oil (solid state, *not melted*)
- 1 tablespoon orange blossom water
- ½ teaspoon vanilla extract
- ½ cup + 1 tablespoon milk
- ¼ cup candied orange peels, chopped

Instructions:

1. Scones take what nineteenth-century bakers like Flora called a "hot oven," so preheat your oven to 425°.
2. Combine the flour, sugar, baking powder, salt, nutmeg, and coconut in a large bowl.
3. Add the coconut oil and use your fingers to massage it into the mixture until the oil is distributed throughout. The mixture should have the appearance of rough sand scooped from Amelia Island's dazzling ocean beach.
4. In a separate bowl, stir the orange blossom water and vanilla into the milk then slowly pour the liquid mixture into the dry mixture, turning it with a spoon until the dough comes together. It will be sticky.
5. Gently fold the candied orange peels into the dough.
6. Turn the dough out onto a well-floured surface. Knead it until it's coated with flour and the surface is smooth, but take care not to overwork it.
7. Divide the dough into two equal parts and press each portion into a round about 3/4-inch thick. Cut each round into 4 wedges and place the wedges on a baking sheet 1 inch apart.
8. Bake for 12-15 minutes or until firm with golden tops. Cool for at least 30 minutes before serving.

Candied Orange Peels

Makes 16 peels

Ingredients:

- 1 large, ripe orange
- 2 cups water
- ½ cup sugar

Instructions:

1. Using a paring knife, slice off the top and bottom of the orange so each

end is flat. Then quarter the peel by making 4 lengthwise (stem side to blossom side, not across the equator), evenly spaced cuts into the rind, deep enough to touch the fruit inside.
2. Pull off the 4 resulting peels with your fingers, being careful not to tear them.
3. Next, use the knife to divide each peel lengthwise to create 8 narrower peels.
4. Take one peel at a time and, keeping the knife flat and maintaining an even downward pressure along the inner contour of the peel, trim off as much of the bitter white pith as you can.
5. Divide each peel lengthwise once more to yield a total of 16 peels.
6. Place the peels in a small saucepan with 1 cup water and bring to a boil, then reduce the heat and maintain a simmer for 15 minutes. This helps take some bitterness out of the peels.
7. Drain the water (save it to sip as orange peel tea, if you'd like!) but leave the peels in the pan.
8. Add the sugar and the remaining 1 cup water to the peels and bring to a boil then reduce the heat and maintain a gentle simmer, stirring occasionally, until the peels turn translucent and some sugar grit starts collecting at the sides and bottom of the saucepan (about 45-55 minutes). You'll know the peels are close to done when the liquid starts to bubble and foam.
9. Place a cooling rack over a bowl and pour the peels and syrup onto the cooling rack, making sure to aim the liquid into the bowl. Separate and straighten the pieces as quickly as you can.
10. Once the pieces have cooled, cover them with a domed plate and let them stand overnight.

Note: You can use store-bought candied orange peels, but making your own is more fun, easier than you'd think, and, of course, what Flora would do. The candied peels also will keep for up to 3 months if you seal them in a jar (as will the syrup that's generated as a delicious by-product, if sealed and refrigerated), so they can be made far ahead of time.

VIII

Laura Bishop Mysteries

Laura Bishop Mysteries by Grace Topping

Staging is Murder
Staging Wars
Upstaged by Murder

Henery Press

Laura Bishop left a career in I.T. to start her own home staging business—helping homeowners prepare their homes for sale. She thought starting her own business in a new field might be murder, but she didn't expect it to include a body. When things become too stressful, she occasionally pulls out the bottle of Harveys Bristol Cream Sherry she keeps to serve her aunt at Christmastime and has a sip of it herself—but not too often. She's found lots of recipes that call for Harveys, including a wonderful English Sherry Trifle. It's not drinking if it's in dessert. Right?

Grace Topping is a *U.S.A. Today* bestselling author and Agatha nominee. A recovering technical writer and I.T. project manager, she was accustomed to writing lean, boring documents. Let loose to write fiction, she is now creating murder mysteries and killing off characters who remind her of some of the people she dealt with during her career. Fictional revenge is sweet. She is the author of the Laura Bishop Mystery series. Grace is the former vice president of the Chesapeake Chapter of Sisters in Crime (SinC), a steering committee member of the SinC Guppies, and a member of Mystery Writers

THE SECRET INGREDIENT

of America. She lives with her husband in Northern Virginia.

English Sherry Trifle

Serves 10

A trifle can best be described as a dessert that is a *trifle* of this and a *trifle* of that. No two people make it exactly the same, and substitutions abound. Making an English trifle is all about layering ingredients in a deep glass bowl for a beautiful presentation. Alternatively, clear glasses with wide openings can be used to make individual desserts.

Ingredients:

- 9×13 white or yellow cake, baked and cooled (lady fingers or sliced pound cake can be substituted)

- 3 heaping tablespoons seedless red raspberry jam, strawberry preserves, or other fruit spread
- ½ cup Harveys Bristol Cream Sherry or any quality cream sherry (see note below)
- 2 cups sliced fresh fruit (strawberries, peaches, or berries)
- 2 small boxes or one large box of Jell-O (strawberry or favorite flavor)
- Birds Custard Powder or 2 boxes of instant or cooked pudding mix
- 4 cups milk to use in prepared custard
- 1½ cups heavy whipping cream
- 1 teaspoon powdered sugar
- 2 or 3 tablespoons ground nuts, chocolate sprinkles, or berries for decoration

Instructions:

1. A trifle consists of layers of cake, fruit, gelatin (Jell-O), custard, whipped cream, and garnishes.
2. Prepare all the ingredients for the layers in advance of layering. The number of layers will depend on the depth of the bowl used. One layer of each will still make for a nice presentation.
3. Line the bottom of the glass dish with slices of cake. Spread the cake with the jam or preserves. Sprinkle the sherry (or fruit juice) evenly over the cake. Note: Harveys Bristol Cream Sherry (not dry sherry) is commonplace in an English sherry trifle, but liqueurs like Grand Marnier, Frangelico, or Amaretto can be substituted. Fruit juice can also be used for a non-alcoholic version.
4. Arrange the sliced fruit over the cake layer. Refrigerate.
5. Prepare the Jell-O and refrigerate until slightly firm but still pourable. Pour the Jell-O over the cake and fruit. Refrigerate until the Jell-O is firm.
6. Add the custard and refrigerate. Note: It's traditional to use Birds Custard Powder, which can often be found in the international food

section of the grocery store. Follow the directions to prepare 2 pints of custard. Homemade custard or 2 boxes of instant or cooked vanilla pudding mix can be substituted. If using cooked pudding, allow to cool thoroughly before adding the custard layer.
7. Beat the whipping cream with the powdered sugar until peaks form. Spread the whipped cream over the custard layer.
8. For more than one layer of each. Repeat each layer, beginning with cake and fruit. Alternate layers. Refrigerate between adding layers of Jell-O to allow the Jell-O to completely firm before adding the next layer. End with whipped cream. Top with nuts, sprinkles, or berries. Refrigerate.
9. If making the trifle a day in advance, leave off the whipped cream and nuts, sprinkles, or berries and add them just before serving.

IX

Cabin by the Lake Mysteries

Cabin by the Lake Mysteries by Linda Norlander

Death of an Editor
Death of a Starling
Death of a Snow Ghost
Death of a Fox
Death of a Dream Catcher

Level Best Books

Each Cabin by the Lake Mystery takes place in a different Minnesota season. In the summer, Jamie Forest, who fled from New York City to the family cabin in the Northwoods, investigates the death of a small-town editor, in the fall a school shooting, and in the winter the death of a new mother who has escaped from the dangers in Central America. During her first spring, she investigates a death in an abandoned T.B. sanitarium. For her second summer, Jamie finds herself investigating a drowning that happened fifteen years before. Along the way, readers experience cabin living through Jamie's eyes. The series includes intrigue, humor, and a wonderful rescue dog named Bronte.

Linda Norlander has written award-winning fiction and nonfiction. In her career as a nurse, she promoted excellence in end-of-life care and authored the award-winning book for nurses entitled, *To Comfort Always: A Nurse's Guide to End-of-Life Care*. She has also won a number of awards for short humor and short fiction. Her Cabin by the Lake series is her first full-length mystery series. While she claims no awards for her cooking, she has been told Jamie's Hearty Beef and Vegetable Stew is delicious and a great meal for a cold winter night. Norlander currently resides in Tacoma, Washington.

Jamie's Hearty Beef Stew and Vegetables

Comfort Food on a Cold Winter's Night
Serves 4-6

Ingredients:

- 2 tablespoons cooking oil
- 1 pound beef stew meat
- 3 tablespoons flour
- 1 large yellow onion
- 1 cup small whole white mushrooms
- 2½ cups beef broth
- 1 cup dry red wine

- 1 teaspoon salt
- ½ teaspoon pepper
- 1 teaspoon dried thyme
- ½ teaspoon rubbed sage
- ½ teaspoon dried basil
- 1 bay leaf
- 3 large carrots cut into ¾-inch slices
- 2 medium red potatoes with skin on cut into one-inch cubes
- 1 cup sliced green beans
- 2 medium parsnips peeled and sliced
- 1 ten-ounce package frozen Brussel sprouts

Variation:

- Add one cup shredded cabbage with the carrots

Instructions:

1. Heat Dutch oven and add cooking oil
2. Dredge beef in flour and brown in Dutch oven for 5 minutes, then add onion and mushrooms. Continue browning until onion is soft.
3. Add beef broth, wine, salt, pepper, thyme, sage, basil, and bay leaf. Simmer for 50 minutes.
4. Add carrots and potatoes and continue simmering for 30 more minutes.
5. Add green beans and parsnips. Continue simmering for 15 minutes.
6. Add Brussel sprouts and simmer for 15 minutes.
7. Serve with heated or toasted garlic bread.

X

Haunted Library Mysteries

Haunted Library Mysteries by Allison Brook

Death Overdue
Read and Gone
Buried in the Stacks
Checked Out for Murder
Death on the Shelf
Dewey Decimated
Book 7 - Title TBD

Crooked Lane Books

The Haunted Library mystery series takes place in Clover Ridge, Connecticut. Thirty-year-old Carrie Singleton is about to turn down the position of Head of Programs and Events at the Clover Ridge Library and resume her nomadic life when Evelyn Havers, the library's resident ghost, advises her to reconsider. Carrie decides to take the job and finds herself involved in murder investigations, many of which have links to cold cases. Evelyn is her able assistant, unless one of her relatives is a suspect. As Carrie gains confidence in her new position, she makes friendships and finds romance, changing the course of her life in a positive way.

A former Spanish teacher, Marilyn Levinson writes mysteries, romantic suspense, and novels for children. Her books have received many accolades. As Allison Brook, she writes the Haunted Library series. *Death Overdue*, the first in the series, was an Agatha nominee for Best Contemporary Novel in 2018. Other mysteries include the Golden Age of Mystery Book Club series and the Twin Lakes series. Her juvenile novel, *Rufus and Magic Run Amok*, was an International Reading Association-Children's Book Council Children's Choice. And *Don't Bring Jeremy* was a nominee for six state awards.

Marilyn lives on Long Island, where many of her books take place.

Marilyn's Veggie and Cheese Casserole

Serves 2-3

Cooking is more forgiving than baking when it comes to precise amounts of ingredients. I never measure when I make casseroles and soups, so my amounts are approximate and can be changed.

Ingredients:

- Cooking spray
- ½ fresh broccoli or cauliflower
- 3 tablespoons olive oil
- ½ red pepper—cut into small pieces

- 3-4 mushrooms—cut into small pieces
- ½ large onion—cut into small pieces
- 3-4 eggs, beaten
- ½ cup panko bread crumbs
- ¾ cup shredded Colby/Monterey cheese
- Parsley or cilantro
- Salt, pepper, red pepper flakes to taste
- Garlic powder
- 4 tablespoons Parmesan cheese

Instructions:

1. Spray a 1½- or 2-quart ceramic casserole dish (at least 3 inches deep) with cooking spray.
2. Set the oven to 350°.
3. Wash and cut up broccoli or cauliflower into small florets. You should get around 2 cups.
4. Microwave in small amount of water for 5 minutes. Drain and add to casserole dish.
5. Put oil in skillet and sauté red pepper 3-4 minutes.
6. Add mushrooms and onion for another 5 minutes or until vegetables are softened. Add to casserole dish.
7. To vegetables add and mix well: Eggs, Bread crumbs, Shredded cheese, Parsley or cilantro, Salt, pepper, red pepper flakes, Garlic powder
8. Sprinkle Parmesan cheese over top.
9. Bake 35-45 minutes uncovered until eggs are set.

XI

Tory Benning Mystery Series

Tory Benning Mysteries by Judith Gonda

Murder in the Secret Maze
Murder in the Christmas Tree Lot
Murder in the Community Garden

Beyond the Page Publishing

Welcome to the California coastal community of Santa Sofia, where landscape architect Tory Benning knows the lay of the land but has to dig through the clues to solve perplexing murders. She'll follow a harrowing path of twists and turns in *Murder in the Secret Maze,* wade through the dizzying aisles of firs and false clues in *Murder in the Christmas Tree Lot,* and comb through a patchwork of plots in *Murder in the Community Garden.* Along with her feisty attorney friend, a heartthrob PI, and a local police detective—not to mention her loyal security detail, a Pomeranian and a black cat—landscape architect Tory Benning brings a whole new meaning to plants and plots in her quest to nab some of California's most cunning criminals.

Judith Gonda is a mystery writer and Ph.D. psychologist with a penchant for Pomeranians and puns, so it's not surprising psychology, Poms, and puns pop up in her amateur sleuth mysteries featuring landscape architect Tory Benning.

Uncle Bob's Christmas Trifle

Serves 8-10

Ingredients:

- 1 orange
- 2 bananas
- Sara Lee family size frozen pound cake–thawed
- 1 15-ounce can sliced pears in fruit juice
- 1 15-ounce can sliced peaches in fruit juice
- 1 bottle Harveys Bristol Cream sherry
- 1 jar raspberry preserves
- 1 large package instant vanilla pudding mix

UNCLE BOB'S CHRISTMAS TRIFLE

- 1 cup milk
- 1 cup eggnog
- 1 cup whipping cream
- 1 tablespoon powdered sugar
- A dash of cinnamon
- A dash of nutmeg
- 1 can whipped cream (like Reddi Wip)
- 2 kiwis
- 1 pint strawberries or raspberries

Instructions:

1. Peel and slice orange and bananas into bite-sized pieces.
2. Slice pound cake into ¼-inch slices.
3. Marinate orange and banana slices and drained pear and peach slices in ½ cup of sherry.
4. Coat the sides and bottom of a deep glass trifle or souffle´ bowl with the raspberry preserves.
5. Drain the sherry from the fruit marinade into a cup after 15-20 minutes.
6. Sprinkle the drained sherry with a spoon over the pound cake.
7. Mix vanilla pudding with the milk and eggnog.
8. Whip the whipping cream, adding powdered sugar to taste.
9. Combine pudding and whipping cream, seasoning with a dash of cinnamon and nutmeg.
10. Line bottom and sides of bowl with pound cake.
11. Sprinkle extra sherry if desired.
12. Spoon some of pudding mixture over the layer of pound cake.
13. Spoon layer of marinated fruit over pudding layer.
14. Repeat layer of pound cake, sherry, preserves (if desired), pudding mixture, and fruit.
15. Cover the top layer with the canned whipped cream.
16. Peel and slice kiwi and strawberries.

17. Top off trifle by alternating kiwi and strawberry slices (or whole raspberries) around the edge of the bowl, continuing until the whole top is covered with red and green fruit for a festive presentation.

XII

All-Day Breakfast Café Mysteries

All-Day Breakfast Café Mysteries by Lena Gregory

Scone Cold Killer
Murder Made to Order
Cold Brew Killing
A Waffle Lot of Murder
Whole Latte Murder
Mistletoe Cake Murder

Lyrical Press

For Florida diner owner Gia Morelli, there's no such thing as too much breakfast—unless it kills you...

When Gia's marriage falls apart, she knows it's time to get out of New York. Her husband was a scam artist who swindled half the millionaires in town, and she doesn't want to be there when they decide to take revenge. On the spur of the moment, she follows her best friend to a small town in Central Florida, where she braves snakes, bears, and giant spiders to open a cheery little diner called the All-Day Breakfast Café. Owning a restaurant has been her lifelong dream, but it turns into a nightmare the morning she opens her dumpster and finds her ex-husband crammed inside. As the suspect du jour, Gia will have to scramble fast to prove her innocence before a killer orders another cup of murder...

Lena Gregory is the author of the Bay Island Psychic Mysteries, which take place on a small island between the north and south forks of Long Island, New York, and the All-Day Breakfast Café Mysteries, which are set on the outskirts of Florida's Ocala National Forest.

Lena grew up in a small town on the south shore of eastern Long Island, but she recently traded in cold, damp, gray winters for the warmth and sunshine of central Florida, where she now lives with her husband, three kids, son-in-law, and four dogs. Her hobbies include spending time with family, reading, and walking. Her love for writing developed when her youngest son was born and didn't sleep through the night. She works full time as a writer and a freelance editor and is a member of Sisters in Crime.

To learn more about Lena and her latest writing endeavors, visit her website at http://www.lenagregory.com.

Gia's Home Fries

Serves 8

Ingredients:

- 1 pound bacon
- 1 large onion
- 1 large green bell pepper
- 5 pounds potatoes
- Salt and pepper (optional – to taste)
- Olive oil or cooking spray (if desired in place of bacon fat)

Instructions:

1. Cook bacon in a large, deep frying pan, drain and set aside. Keep fat in frying pan.
2. Finely dice onion and green pepper. Add to frying pan with bacon fat (*For a healthier version, you can substitute cooking spray or coat the bottom of a frying pan with olive oil) and cook until just tender.
3. Peel and chop potatoes into small pieces. (Best if all the pieces are around the same size.)
4. Add potatoes to pan.
5. Crumble bacon into potatoes (minus one piece to eat, because, well, it's bacon!), stir, and cover.
6. Cook on medium heat, stirring occasionally, until potatoes are tender, about 30-35 minutes.
7. Salt and pepper to taste. Serve with any style eggs and enjoy!

XIII

Cupcake Catering Mystery Series

Cupcake Catering Mysteries by Kim Davis

Sprinkles of Suspicion
Cake Popped Off
Framed and Frosted

Cinnamon & Sugar Press

Featuring Emory Martinez, the Cupcake Catering Mystery series follows Emory as she develops from an insecure accountant to a murder suspect to an amateur sleuth. After facing arrest and losing her husband, her job, and her home, with the help of octogenarian Tillie Skyler, Emory launches her delicious new cupcake catering business while solving murders. Along the way, she bakes up scrumptious treats to share with family and friends. Recipes are included with each book.

Kim Davis lives in Southern California with her husband. When not chasing her two granddaughters, she can be found at her computer writing or blogging at Cinnamon, Sugar, and a Little Bit of Murder or in the kitchen baking up new treats to share. Kim Davis is a member of Sisters in Crime and Mystery Writers of America.

Tropical Pineapple Muffins

Makes 16 muffins

Being responsible for cooking meals for Tillie, her octogenarian employer, Emory likes to serve muffins for an easy breakfast. She often makes a variety of batches ahead of time and then, once completely cooled, wraps individual muffins in plastic wrap and stores them in the freezer. This gives Emory and Tillie more time to linger over coffee, with an extra muffin, as they solve murders or come up with crazy cocktail-flavored cupcakes recipes.

Ingredients:

- 1 cup crushed pineapple, well-drained

TROPICAL PINEAPPLE MUFFINS

- 1¾ cups all-purpose flour
- 2 teaspoons baking powder
- 1 teaspoon salt
- ¾ cup granulated sugar
- ¾ cup sweetened coconut flakes (divided)
- 2 eggs
- ½ cup non-dairy coconut milk beverage
- 2 tablespoons coconut oil, melted
- Pineapple
- ¼ cup pineapple juice from drained
- 2 teaspoons vanilla extract

Instructions:

1. Heat oven to 350°. Line muffin tins with paper cupcake liners and set aside.
2. Drain the crushed pineapple well and reserve ¼ cup juice. Set aside.
3. In a large bowl, whisk together the flour, baking powder, salt, and sugar then stir in ½ cup coconut flakes. Set aside.
4. In a medium bowl, whisk together eggs, coconut milk, melted coconut oil, pineapple, reserved pineapple juice, and vanilla. To melt coconut oil, place coconut oil in a microwave-safe bowl and heat at 50% power for 30 seconds. Stir and repeat heating as necessary until melted, before adding to bowl.
5. Make a well in the center of the dry ingredients then pour the wet ingredients in and stir together until combined.
6. Fill the muffin tin cups ¾ full then divide remaining ¼ cup coconut flakes and sprinkle over the top of the batter.
7. Bake 18–20 minutes. The tops should turn golden and the muffins spring back when lightly pressed.
8. Remove from oven and cool in the cupcake tin for 5 minutes. Remove the muffins from the pan and cool on a wire rack.

9. Store leftovers in an airtight container for up to 2 days. To store longer, wrap cooled muffins individually in plastic wrap then place in a freezer-safe Ziploc bag. Refrigerate until thoroughly chilled then store in the freezer. Allow plastic-wrapped muffins to defrost at room temperature for a few hours, or overnight.

Choco-Colada Cocktail Cupcakes

Makes 18-20 cupcakes

As Emory's cupcake catering business expands, her octogenarian employer, Tillie, likes to scour Pinterest to find unique cocktails and challenge Emory to turn them into cupcakes that mimic the taste. Tillie's bridge club members request Choco-Colada Cocktail Cupcakes often, since the rich, fudgy frosting and cupcakes combine favorite flavors of chocolate, coffee, and coconut. The added rum to the frosting hints at a boozy kick.

Cupcakes Ingredients:

- 1 15.25-ounce box chocolate cake mix

- 3 eggs
- ½ cup vegetable oil
- ½ teaspoon coconut extract
- ¼ cup + 1 tablespoon gold rum
- ¼ cup Kahlua
- ¼ cup dark Crème de Cacao
- ¼ cup Coco Lopez (or Cream of Coconut)
- ¼ cup half-and-half *

***Note**

If your boxed cake mix calls for less than 1¼ cups of water, decrease half-and-half to 1 tablespoon. Different brands of cake mix call for different liquid measurements.

Frosting Ingredients:

- ⅓ cup gold rum
- ½ teaspoon instant powdered coffee (such as Starbucks' Via)
- ⅛ teaspoon salt
- ½ teaspoon coconut extract
- 2 cups (12 ounces) semi-sweet chocolate chips
- ¼ cup unsalted butter
- 2 tablespoons half-and-half
- 1 tablespoon corn syrup
- 2½ cups (11.2 ounces) confectioners' sugar

Cupcakes Instructions:

1. Preheat oven to 350°.
2. Line cupcake tins with paper liners.
3. Place cake mix in a large mixing bowl and add the remaining ingredients.

CHOCO-COLADA COCKTAIL CUPCAKES

4. Using an electric mixer, beat on low speed for 30 seconds then increase speed to medium-high and beat for 2 minutes.
5. Fill cupcake liners 3/4 full and bake 15–21 minutes. (Baking time will vary depending on brand of cake mix used.) When done, cupcake tops will spring back when lightly touched or a wooden skewer inserted into center will come out mostly clean. A few moist crumbs clinging is okay.
6. Remove from oven and allow to cool in the cupcake tin for 5 minutes.
7. Move the cupcakes to a wire rack and cool completely before applying the frosting.

Frosting Instructions:

1. Combine rum, powdered coffee, salt, and coconut extract in a small microwave-safe dish.
2. Heat the mixture 30 seconds in microwave until liquid is hot enough to dissolve the coffee. Stir well then set aside.
3. Combine chocolate chips, butter, half-and-half, and corn syrup in a large microwave-safe bowl.
4. Heat chocolate mixture in microwave on high power for 1 minute.
5. Remove from microwave and vigorously stir then continue heating and stirring in 20 second increments until butter and chips are melted. Be sure to stir after each heat cycle so the chocolate doesn't scorch. Mixture may look grainy but will smooth out as you whisk in remaining ingredients.
6. Once the chocolate is melted, whisk in the rum mixture.
7. Add the confectioners' sugar and stir until smooth. If the frosting is too thick, add additional half-and-half, ½ teaspoon at a time, until desired consistency is reached.
8. Frost the cupcakes while the frosting is still warm. If the frosting thickens as it cools and is difficult to spread, reheat for a few seconds in the microwave.
9. Garnish with toasted coconut.

Garnish Suggestion

- ⅓ cup toasted coconut

To toast coconut, place in a small skillet over medium-low heat. Stirring constantly, cook until the coconut is lightly browned. Immediately transfer the toasted coconut onto a cool plate to keep from over-cooking. Allow to completely cool before garnishing the cupcakes.

Choco-Colada Cocktail

Serves 1

On its own or served with Choco-Colada Cocktail Cupcakes, this sweet dessert libation is sure to tempt your taste buds.

Ingredients:

- ½ ounce gold rum (or substitute Malibu rum for more coconut flavor)
- ½ ounce Kahlua
- ½ ounce dark Crème de Cacoa
- ½ ounce Coco Lopez (or Cream of Coconut)
- 2 ounces half-and-half

Garnish:

- Your favorite chocolate syrup
- Whipped cream
- Toasted coconut

Instructions:

1. If garnishing, prior to mixing cocktail, dip the rim of the cocktail glass into your favorite chocolate syrup.
2. Turn the glass right side up, allowing the syrup to drip down the sides. Refrigerate until ready.
3. Place all the cocktail ingredients into an ice-filled shaker.
4. Vigorously shake until thoroughly chilled then strain into the prepared glass.
5. Swirl whipped cream over the top and sprinkle with toasted coconut, if desired.

XIV

Low Country Dog Walker Mysteries

Low Country Dog Walker Mysteries by Jackie Layton

Bite the Dust
Dog-Gone Dead
Bag of Bones

Bell Bridge Books

Bark and Seek
Run with the Big Dogs
Hot Doggin'

Beyond the Page Publishing

Andi Grace Scott loves dogs and her South Carolina life in the low country. She's never met a dog she didn't like, and she has a knack for matching stray dogs with people. Andi Grace starts sleuthing when she finds a dead body and the police suspect her. She's determined to prove her innocence and find justice for the victim.

In the Low Country Dog Walker Mystery series, Andi Grace questions many of the locals and visits southern plantations, coffee shops, pizza parlors, antique shops, beaches, and other areas along the South Carolina coast. If you enjoy small-town life and fun characters, you'll enjoy reading this series.

Jackie Layton has many happy memories of baking with her mother. Thanksgiving was the season for baking pies, and Christmas was the time for baking cookies. They used old family recipes from both sides of the family. They even baked Springerle cookies, a German cookie made with special molds brought here when Jackie's father's family came to the United States.

Andi Grace Scott's Puppy Chow

Serves 10

Ingredients:

- 3 cups Wheat Chex
- 3 cups Rice Chex
- 3 cups Cinnamon Chex
- 1 cup peanut butter
- 1 cup semi-sweet chocolate chips
- 1 cup pecans (Because Southern girls love pecans)
- 1 teaspoon cinnamon sugar
- 1½ cups confectioners' sugar

Alternate ingredients:

- Use almond butter instead of peanut butter.
- Add M&Ms right before serving for an extra chocolate boost.

Instructions:

1. Mix the Chex cereals in a bowl and set aside.
2. Melt peanut butter and chocolate chips in microwave-safe bowl for 30 seconds at a time and stir. Continue this until the mixture is smooth and shiny.
3. In a big bowl add 1 cup of the Chex mix and pour some of the peanut butter and chocolate chip mixture on top. Stir.
4. Add pecans and cinnamon sugar. Stir.
5. Add more cereal and peanut butter and chocolate chip mixture and stir. Continue this until all ingredients are used.
6. Allow the mixture to cool slightly.
7. When the mixture reaches room temperature, stir in confectioners' sugar ¼ cup at a time to taste.
8. Stir gently until all of the mixture is coated.
9. Allow to cool more and add more confectioners' sugar to taste.
10. Serve at room temperature.

Juliet's Chocolate Bars

Makes 12-15 bars

Bars Ingredients:

- 1 stick butter, softened
- 1 cup sugar
- 4 eggs
- 1 cup flour
- 1 teaspoon baking powder
- 1 teaspoon pure vanilla
- 16 ounces Hershey's chocolate syrup

Frosting Ingredients:

- 3 squares Baker's Semi Sweet Baking Chocolate Bar
- ¾ stick butter
- 2⅔ cup confectioners' sugar
- 1 teaspoon vanilla
- Milk
- Optional-chopped pecans

Bars Instructions:

1. Preheat oven to 350°.
2. Cream butter and sugar. Add one egg at a time and beat.
3. In another bowl, mix flour and baking powder then slowly stir this mixture into the butter, sugar, and egg mixture.
4. Add vanilla and chocolate syrup.
5. Mix well and pour into a greased and floured 9x13 pan.
6. Bake 30 minutes.

Frosting Instructions:

1. After the cake is cool, in a double boiler, melt chocolate and butter.
2. When melted, add to confectioners' sugar then add vanilla.
3. Stir in small amounts of milk until smooth.
4. Add pecans at this point and stir again.
5. Frost the cake.
6. It's best to serve this as a sheet cake because the cake and frosting are thick.

Marc's Sunshine Smoothie

Serves 1

Ingredients:

- 8 ounces Greek vanilla yogurt
- 1 cup chilled orange juice
- ⅛ teaspoonful ground cinnamon
- ¼ cup strawberries
- ¼ cup blueberries
- 6 ice cubes

Instructions:

1. Toss all ingredients into blender and process until smooth.
2. Drink immediately.

This is especially refreshing after a morning run.

XV

Jules Keene Glamping Mysteries

Jules Keene Glamping Mysteries by Heather Weidner

Vintage Trailers and Blackmailers
Film Crews and Rendezvous
Christmas Lights and Catfights

Level Best Books

Jules Keene spends most of her days trying to keep her resort profitable and competitive in a world with so many vacation options. The former campground, set in the heart of Virginia's Blue Ridge Mountains near Charlottesville in the quaint town of Fern Valley, offers guests a unique vacation in refurbished and upcycled vintage trailers. Hoping to expand her offerings, she partners with her maintenance guy to create a village of tiny houses, part of the latest D.I.Y. craze, to give her guests another unique vacation option.

If trying to keep the resort solvent wasn't enough, murder finds its way to the sleepy, one-stoplight town, and Jules is thrust in the middle of the mayhem when she helps the local sheriff solve the crimes before they destroy her business.

Jules, the busy entrepreneur, often doesn't have a lot of time to cook. She likes good food that's easy to prepare, like this cool dessert, good any season.

Heather Weidner also writes the Delanie Fitzgerald mystery series set in Virginia (*Secret Lives and Private Eyes, The Tulip Shirt Murders,* and *Glitter, Glam, and Contraband*). Her short stories appear in the Virginia is for Mysteries series, *50 Shades of Cabernet,* and *Deadly Southern Charm.* Her novellas appear in The Mutt Mysteries series.

Originally from Virginia Beach, Heather has been a mystery fan since *Scooby-Doo* and *Nancy Drew.* She lives in Central Virginia with her husband and a pair of Jack Russell terriers. She is a member of Sisters in Crime–Central Virginia, Sisters in Crime–Chessie, Guppies, International Thriller Writers, and James River Writers.

Through the years, she has been a cop's kid, technical writer, editor, college professor, software tester, and I.T. manager.

Chocolaty Éclair Pies

Serves 6-8

Ingredients:

- 2 4-ounce packages French vanilla instant pudding
- 3 cups milk
- 1 12-ounce container whipped topping (Creamy Cool Whip works best)
- 1 box plain graham crackers (no cinnamon)
- 1 package chocolate icing

Instructions:

1. Prepare the pudding according to the package directions but use the milk.
2. Mix the pudding and the whipped topping together.
3. In a 9x13 pan or dish, cover the bottom with graham crackers. (You may have to break the crackers to fill the entire bottom of the pan.)
4. Pour half of the pudding mixture on top of the cookies and spread it evenly in the pan. Top with another layer of graham crackers.
5. Then pour the other half of the pudding and spread evenly.
6. Cover the second layer of pudding with another layer of graham crackers.
7. Ice the top layer of graham crackers.
8. This is best if you can refrigerate it overnight to soften the graham crackers. Cut and serve.
9. For fun, you can use food coloring to dye the vanilla pudding/whipped topping mixture.

XVI

Washington Whodunit Mysteries

Washington Whodunit Mysteries by Colleen J. Shogan

Stabbing in the Senate
Homicide in the House
Calamity at the Continental Club
K Street Killing
Gore in the Garden
Larceny at the Library
Dead as a Duck

Camel Press

The Washington Whodunit mystery series is set in our nation's capital and features Kit Marshall, a thirty-something congressional staffer who finds out the hard way politics can be murder. Kit solves crimes in Washington, D.C., along with a plucky band of friends and her chubby beagle mutt Clarence. Kit also manages to find her way into the most fascinating sites in the city, including the Smithsonian, Mount Vernon, the National Archives, the Botanic Garden, and the Library of Congress.

Stabbing in the Senate was awarded the Next Generation Indie prize for Best Mystery in 2016. *Homicide in the House* was a 2017 finalist for the RONE Award for Best Mystery. *Calamity at the Continental Club* was a 2018 finalist in the "best cozy mystery" at Killer Nashville. *Larceny at the Library* won the bronze medal for "best ebook mystery" at the IPPY Awards.

Colleen J. Shogan has been reading mysteries since the age of six. She conceived of the plot of her first novel one morning while taking a walk in her suburban Washington, D.C., neighborhood. A political scientist by training, Colleen has taught American politics at numerous universities. She previously worked on Capitol Hill as a legislative staffer in the United States Senate and as a senior executive at the Library of Congress. Currently, she's the Senior Vice President at the White House Historical Association. Colleen lives in Arlington, Virginia, and Duck, N.C., with her husband, Rob, and their beagle mutt Conan. She is a member of Sisters in Crime.

Pepperoni Bread

Serves 6

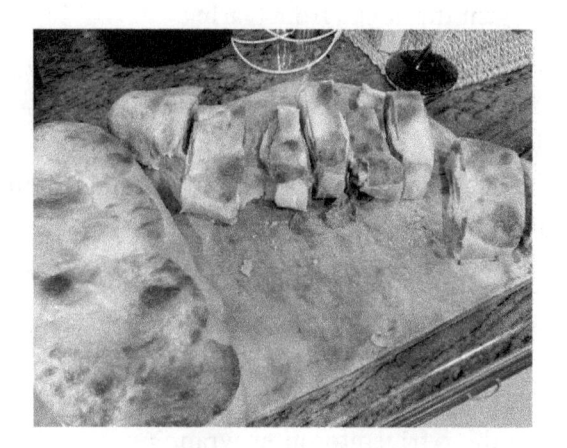

Ingredients:

- Cooking spray
- 1 package refrigerated classic pizza crust dough (Pillsbury or any other brand is fine)
- 4-6 ounces pepperoni, sliced and cut up into small pieces
- 8 oz. shredded mozzarella cheese
- 8 oz. sliced provolone (about 8 generous slices)
- Olive oil

Instructions:

1. Spray a baking or cookie sheet with cooking spray
2. Preheat oven to 400°.
3. Roll out pizza crust onto the cookie sheet. Don't stretch it too thin.
4. Spread the pepperoni on top of the dough. Make sure the pepperoni covers the entire dough, including the corners.
5. Spread the entire amount of mozzarella on top of the pepperoni, once again making sure the cheese covers the entirety of the rolled-out dough.
6. Place slices of provolone on top of the mozzarella, reserving 2 slices.
7. Carefully roll up the dough lengthwise, like a jelly roll. You need to roll slowly to prevent the dough from tearing.
8. Close up the ends of the roll.
9. Brush the roll lightly with olive oil.
10. Make shallow cuts at an angle on the top of the roll.
11. Place the half slices of provolone on top of the roll, in between the shallow cuts.
12. Place in heated oven for 25-30 minutes. Watch it to make sure it doesn't burn.
13. After removing the roll from the oven, let it cool for 10 minutes.
14. Slice the pepperoni roll and serve immediately. Or place the unsliced baked roll in the refrigerator after wrapping it in foil. Slices can be reheated in the oven or microwave.

Kit really likes this recipe because it's easy to make and delicious. She serves it to Doug and her friends as a hearty appetizer. It pairs well with beer, red wine, or soda. It's also one of Clarence's favorites, since he's obsessed with pepperoni!

Acknowledgements

This project was conceived by our extraordinary agent, Dawn Dowdle. We are grateful for her passion of our books, our characters, and our recipes. Thanks also to Level Best Books for their energetic support.